T0378706

Exploring Solutions

GUN VIOLENCE

Jennifer Stephan

San Diego, CA

About the Author

Jennifer Stephan writes nonfiction books and articles for tweens and teens. Her work explores how people change and are changed by the communities and times in which they live. She earned a PhD in human development and social policy from Northwestern University and has worked as an education policy researcher. She lives outside Chicago with her husband and daughters.

© 2024 ReferencePoint Press, Inc.
Printed in the United States

For more information, contact:
ReferencePoint Press, Inc.
PO Box 27779
San Diego, CA 92198
www.ReferencePointPress.com

ALL RIGHTS RESERVED.
No part of this work covered by the copyright hereon may be reproduced or used in any form or by any means—graphic, electronic, or mechanical, including photocopying, recording, taping, web distribution, or information storage retrieval systems—without the written permission of the publisher.

LIBRARY OF CONGRESS CATALOGING-IN-PUBLICATION DATA

Names: Stephan, Jennifer, author.
Title: Exploring solutions: gun violence / by Jennifer Stephan.
Description: San Diego, CA : ReferencePoint Press, Inc., [2024] | Series: Exploring solutions | Includes bibliographical references and index.
Identifiers: LCCN 2023000985 (print) | ISBN 9781678205461 (library binding) | ISBN 9781678205478 (ebook)
Subjects: LCSH: gun violence--Juvenile literature

CONTENTS

Introduction   **4**
Moving Beyond Gun Politics

Chapter One   **7**
The Gun Violence Problem

Chapter Two   **17**
Limit Access to Guns Through
Additional Legislation

Chapter Three   **26**
Improve the Enforcement of Gun Laws

Chapter Four   **36**
Implement Programs Targeting
High-Risk Individuals

Chapter Five   **46**
Change the Environment to Change Behavior

Source Notes	56
For Further Research	59
Index	61
Picture Credits	64

INTRODUCTION

Moving Beyond Gun Politics

After another school shooting, this time at an elementary school in Uvalde, Texas, gun safety activist David Hogg fumed. "I'm sick and tired of us giving ourselves pats on the back for trying," he told reporter Charlotte Alter. "Objectively we've been failing."[1] Hogg had been trying to stop gun violence for four years, ever since a shooter tore through his Parkland, Florida, high school in 2018. A lot changed that day. Seventeen people died. The survivors entered a new reality, and Hogg, along with a group of classmates, started a national movement. The teens coordinated a response to the school shooting with a speed, size, and savvy the nation had never seen. At March for Our Lives rallies, the first of which took place just weeks after the mass shooting, Hogg and his peers have railed against lawmakers who oppose strict gun laws. They promised to evict lawmakers from political office if they did not step up. Hogg has called it a battle of "kids vs. evil."[2]

Seeking a New Approach

But after four years, and despite the teens' unprecedented efforts, gun violence has not abated. Mass shootings have increased. As Alter writes, Hogg has come to believe solving gun violence requires a different approach. He now celebrates modest victories and seeks solutions beyond just new laws. Hogg also believes more in compromise. In a June

2022 opinion piece published by Fox News, Hogg appealed directly to conservatives to work with liberals on solutions. "I don't know what the exact answer is, but I know that you should be at the table," he wrote. "Your voice

> "I'm sick and tired of us giving ourselves pats on the back for trying. . . . Objectively we've been failing."[1]
>
> —David Hogg, gun safety activist

matters. Your rights matter. Your decency matters. We have disagreed in the past, but we are not enemies. Our enemy is not a party or organization, it is gun violence."[3] Instead of leading with anger, Hogg is now hoping to work on practical solutions.

Gun policy is a polarizing issue, but gun violence is not. Eighty percent of Americans say it is extremely or very important to reduce all types of gun violence, and most Americans also say it is important to protect the right to own guns, according to a 2022 Associated Press/NORC survey. The Centers for Disease Control and Prevention (CDC) reports that over forty-seven thousand people died from gun violence in 2021. Many more suffered injuries, trauma, and the financial burdens of gun violence. Gun violence takes multiple forms—self-inflicted, interpersonal, and unintentional—that afflict different groups of people differently. People of color, males, and youth suffer disproportionately.

Gun safety activist David Hogg addresses the March for Our Lives rally in Washington, DC, on June 11, 2022.

Violence can spread like a disease. It spreads across peer groups and communities through exposure and fear. "If you live in a place where you don't feel safe, don't feel like the police will help you, and you know other people have guns, it's hard to persuade you you don't need a gun,"[4] says psychiatrist Amy Barnhorst. Gun violence also spreads over time. Today's victim can become tomorrow's offender when violent acts lead to retaliation. Children who experience violence in their homes or communities are at greater risk of becoming violent adults, making the problem intergenerational.

The Need for Solutions

Solutions to gun violence must be as complex and layered as the problem. The traditional approach relies on gun laws and law enforcement. But these powerful tools have become entangled in a political tug-of-war. A newer, public health approach focuses on prevention and changing individuals and environments to reduce violence. This less controversial approach can reduce shootings, but it takes time. People living with the threat of violence need solutions now.

Reducing gun violence will require multiple strategies that address different forms and causes of violence. New legislation and improved law enforcement can limit access to guns for high-risk people. Interventions targeting at-risk individuals and environments address the underlying causes of violence. David Hogg is not the only one ready for a new approach. In June 2022 Congress passed the Bipartisan Safer Communities Act, the first federal gun safety legislation to pass in decades. The legislation may not be as sweeping as some had hoped, but it moves beyond gun politics to actual solutions for reducing gun violence.

CHAPTER ONE

The Gun Violence Problem

Music and laughter bubbled up from a colorfully dressed crowd looping through the streets of Boston for the 2022 Mother's Day Walk for Peace. The annual march is festive but bittersweet. It honors mothers whose children have died from violence and fund-raises to help the community heal. Team Dre'Shaun Johnson, Team Scooby, and Team Dejah walked, like other friends and family, in remembrance of their loved ones' bright smiles and big hearts. They joined religious congregations and not-for-profit organizations. Over the walk's twenty-six years, the crowd has grown. "It's both fabulous and horrible that it's gotten bigger,"[5] says a marcher. Over time, the victims and the calls for peace have accumulated.

Kim Odom marched that day for her son, Steven, who had been shot to death in 2007 as he walked home from a basketball game. It was a case of mistaken identity. Ten days after the thirteen-year-old's murder, crime researcher Thomas Abt reports, the alleged gunman was killed. A few weeks later, another man who had been with the alleged gunman at Steven's murder was shot and paralyzed. The boy who had obtained the gun used to kill Steven was later arrested and sent to prison. Odom did not feel vindicated by what happened to her son's alleged attackers. She felt devastated. "We feel heavy because now there are four families that are suffering the pain from this vicious cycle of violence,"[6] Odom

7

says. Shootings do not just change the lives of victims. The consequences reverberate through families, communities, and time.

The forms, outcomes, and underlying causes of gun violence are multiple and intersecting. Gun violence can be self-inflicted, interpersonal, or unintentional; targeted or random; planned or impulsive; and involve one or more casualties. Gun violence impacts all Americans but not equally. People of different races, genders, and ages experience different forms of gun violence at different rates. Solutions require an understanding of the what and the why of the problem and its physical, mental, and financial costs.

Self-Inflicted, Interpersonal, and Unintentional Gun Violence

In 2021 more than 47,000 people died from a gunshot, according to the CDC. That represents more than 130 lives lost a day. Deaths are the most serious, reported, and reliable indicators of gun violence. Injuries and trauma can remain hidden, but deaths rarely do.

Most gun deaths are suicides. Gun suicide disproportionately impacts White men, older people, and people living in rural areas. But since 2011, gun suicide rates among young people of color have risen the fastest. Some of these lives may have been saved if a gun had not been accessible. Suicidal crises can pass. One study found that almost a quarter of people who survived a severe suicide attempt had deliberated less than five minutes before making the attempt. Most people who attempt suicide do not go on to die by suicide. But guns make attempts highly lethal. Over 80 percent of people who attempt suicide with a gun die. "Even if you were 0% effective at preventing people from attempting suicide, replacing the means—the access to firearms—would save the majority of people,"[7] says Ari Freilich, state policy director at Giffords Law Center, an advocacy organiza-

> "Even if you were 0% effective at preventing people from attempting suicide, replacing the means—the access to firearms—would save the majority of people."[7]
>
> —Ari Freilich, state policy director at Giffords Law Center

The Recent Spike in Gun Violence

Gun homicides jumped 35 percent from 2019 to 2020. That is the largest yearly increase in modern history, according to the Johns Hopkins Center for Gun Violence Solutions. In 2021, gun homicides and gun suicides climbed even higher. No one knows with certainty why gun violence has spiked, but experts speculate that the stress of recent events has heightened aggressive tendencies. Some experts point to mental health and financial strains brought on by the COVID-19 pandemic. Other experts blame the growing political divisiveness linked to the 2020 presidential election and its aftermath. Some suggest that intensifying tensions between police and communities of color over the time period might have limited the effectiveness of policing by eroding public confidence in police or redirecting police resources to manage protests rather than crime. The number of new gun purchases also increased over the same time period. "These are particularly high-stress times," sociologist Nicole Kravitz-Wirtz told the *New York Times*. "When you add a firearm into those situations it adds particularly fatal risk."

Quoted in Thomas Fuller and Tim Arango, "Police Pin a Rise in Murders on an Unusual Suspect: Covid," *New York Times*, November 15, 2021. www.nytimes.com.

tion. People who attempt suicide with a gun do not get time to rethink their decision and rarely get a second chance at life.

In 2022 almost twenty-one thousand people died by gun homicide. Gun homicides often result from arguments, rivalries, or retaliation, or they occur in the process of committing another crime. Males, youth, and people of color die from gun homicide at the highest rates. Black males ages fifteen to thirty-four accounted for 2 percent of Americans in 2020 but 38 percent of all gun homicide victims, according to analysis by Johns Hopkins University. Gun homicides occur at similar rates in urban and rural areas. But because many more people live in cities, urban community violence is highly concentrated. According to the Chicago Police Department, for example, an average of nine shootings occurred in Chicago each day of 2021, and those are just the ones reported to police.

More than five hundred people died from an unintentional gunshot in 2020, according to Johns Hopkins University. Unintentional gun deaths can be self-inflicted or caused by another person. They impact older children, teens, and young adults at the highest rates. One study found that children and teens often die while playing with a gun. Alcohol consumption was suspected in almost half the unintentional deaths of young adults. Gun safety advocates reject labeling these deaths "accidents" because they believe appropriate education, training, and storage could prevent the incidents.

Specific Forms of Interpersonal Violence

Interpersonal gun violence, which occurs between people, can take different forms that may require different solutions. Women accounted for just 16 percent of gun homicide victims in 2021. When women do become victims, it is often at the hands of an intimate partner—a current or former spouse, boyfriend, girlfriend, or co-parent. Guns in domestic abuse situations endanger more than just partners. Relatives, friends, and colleagues have also become victims of domestic violence. In May 2021 Sandra Ibarra-Perez's boyfriend showed up uninvited to a party at her home in Colorado Springs. According to police, the boyfriend had "power and control issues."[8] Angry at not being invited to the party, the man shot and killed Ibarra-Perez and five of her relatives with a semiautomatic pistol. Three young children witnessed the killings. Guns in the hands of abusers also endanger police officers, who consider domestic violence calls among the most hazardous parts of their job.

Mass shootings grab headlines but account for only a tiny fraction of gun deaths. The Gun Violence Archive defines a mass shooting as any incident in which four or more people are injured or killed (not including the shooter). This includes people shot in homes, in public, or during the process of committing a crime. By this broad definition, 705 people died in a mass shooting in 2021. News headlines often focus on shootings of innocent victims that occur in public spaces. These account for even fewer gun deaths. But over time, these public mass shootings have become more frequent and more deadly. Public mass shootings occur most often in the shooter's current or former workplace, according to the Violence Project. They also occur in schools and other

10

Gun-Related Suicides and Homicides, 2021

Rates of gun-related suicides and homicides in the United States in 2021 reached their highest levels since the early 1990s. According to provisional data published by the Centers for Disease Control and Prevention (CDC), an estimated 26,320 firearm suicides and 20,966 firearm homicides took place in 2021.

Source: Thomas R. Simon et al., "Notes from the Field: Increases in Firearm Homicide and Suicide Rates—United States, 2020–2021," *Morbidity and Mortality Weekly Report*, October 7, 2022. www.cdc.gov.

locations, such as houses of worship or nightclubs. Such shootings may seem impulsive and random, but about half of public mass shooters engage in medium to high levels of planning, and they sometimes target particular types of victims. In May 2022, for example, a shooter killed ten Black people at a grocery store in Buffalo, New York, because of their race.

When gun violence occurs, victims often turn to the police. Sometimes the police are the offenders. The *Washington Post* estimates that police shot and killed over one thousand people in 2021. Some shootings are justified, but others are questionable. A *New York Times* investigation found that officers shot and killed four hundred unarmed drivers or passengers in traffic stops over a five-year period. Black Americans are much more likely to die by police gunfire than White Americans.

The Cost of School Security

The aftermath of gun violence costs money. So does its prevention. School systems and colleges spent over $3.1 billion on security products and services in 2021, according to analysis by technology research company Omdia. This includes low-tech solutions like lockdown window shades and supply kits for classrooms or bulletproof whiteboards. Sophisticated security solutions include gun-detection systems that scan security camera footage for firearms in real time, wireless alert systems used by staff to communicate in a crisis, facial recognition systems that detect whether a stranger has entered a school, and technology that allows local police to remotely control school security cameras, the public announcement system, and door locks.

Some experts think the spending on school security has gone too far. Although tragic, school shootings are relatively rare. Sophisticated school security measures are costly and do not always work as expected. Critics also worry that surveillance technologies threaten privacy and undermine healthy adult-adolescent relationships that serve as a protective factor against gun violence.

Gun violence takes various forms that impact different groups of people at different rates. People who are older, White, or living in rural areas die from gun suicide at the highest rates. Youth and people of color die from gun homicide at the highest rates. Males die from gun homicide much more often than females. Although relatively fewer people die in mass or unintentional shootings or at the hands of an intimate partner or police officer, these forms of gun violence have unique dimensions that solutions cannot ignore.

Injuries and Trauma

Gun violence does not just cause death. Its outcomes are multifarious and far reaching, something the residents of Highland Park, Illinois, know well. The whole town, it seems, shows up for Highland Park's annual July 4 parade. In 2022 lawn chairs and strollers lined the sidewalks, and families decked out in red, white, and blue were cheering for friends and neighbors marching by. Eight-year-old Cooper Roberts was there with his family. They had snagged a prime spot close to Walker Bros. restaurant. At 10:14 a.m., the lives of these parade goers changed forever. A gunman unleashed more than eighty bullets from a nearby rooftop, killing seven people and injuring dozens. One bullet struck Cooper's spinal cord, paralyzing him from the waist down. After eleven weeks in the hospital and then rehab, Cooper returned home. He cannot ride a bike, play soccer, or climb playground equipment. For every gun death, gun violence causes an estimated two to three injuries, according to data from the National Center for Injury Prevention and Control. Some victims heal physically with time, but others suffer chronic pain and disabilities.

Experiencing or witnessing violence is also associated with poor mental health outcomes. When a bullet paralyzed Cooper Roberts, it was not just his physical health that suffered. "Cooper has to deal on a daily basis with the sadness and grief of recognizing all the things he's lost—all that he used to be able to do at his house, in his community, that he cannot do anymore,"[9] say Cooper's parents, Jason and Keely Roberts. Harvard Medical School researchers found that people who sustained a gun injury experienced a 51 percent increase in psychiatric disorders and an 85 percent increase in substance use disorders compared to similar people without a gun injury. It was not just the victims who struggled mentally. Their family members also experienced psychiatric disorders at higher rates. Just hearing about violence can strain mental health. A 2018 Harris poll found that mass shootings represent a significant source of stress for most teens and parents.

In some urban communities the seeming indifference of Americans compounds the trauma from gun violence. Alvoncia Jackson, who lives in Washington, DC, lost her grandson to gun homicide in 2022. "The two mass shootings that just happened gained attention around the world," she says. "But when it's a shooting on a city street, nothing happens. . . . Nobody is standing to speak for us."[10] The

> "Cooper has to deal on a daily basis with the sadness and grief of recognizing all the things he's lost—all that he used to be able to do at his house, in his community, that he cannot do anymore."[9]
>
> —Jason and Keely Roberts, parents of mass shooting survivor

effects of shootings on mental health depend on the recency, frequency, intensity, and proximity of the violence and the resources people have to help them cope.

Economic Consequences

Americans pay a high price for gun violence. Medical expenses for gun injuries cost Americans an estimated $630 million in 2010, according to research by the Urban Institute. For families, the costs of funerals, doctors, hospitals, or therapists coupled with missed work can turn a physical and emotional tragedy into a financial challenge. Gun violence also imposes costs on taxpayers, who not only cover a significant share of medical bills but also pay for the prosecution of gun crimes and incarceration.

Over time, concentrated gun violence can impoverish whole communities. It discourages new businesses from coming into affected areas and reduces the profitability of current businesses. When people feel afraid to shop or businesses shorten their hours to avoid violence, revenues fall. Extra security such as cameras, bulletproof glass, or guards raise business expenses. If low profits force local businesses to close, local jobs disappear. The Urban Institute estimates that each gun homicide in an Oakland,

Among the burdens on taxpayers is the cost of housing perpetrators of gun violence in prisons. Prisoners are shown at the Federal Correctional Institution building in Los Angeles, California.

California, neighborhood corresponded to a loss of five jobs in Oakland, California, whereas in Minneapolis, Minnesota, a loss of eighty jobs corresponded to each homicide. When residents and businesses leave a community, local tax revenues fall, making it more difficult for cities to provide policing and support services to residents who stay. The communities most impacted by ongoing gun violence are often those least able to afford the loss of businesses, jobs, and tax revenue. Gun violence causes more than death. Injuries, trauma, and financial difficulties can last a lifetime.

Risk Factors for Gun Violence

The causes of gun violence are complex and not completely understood, but research has identified factors that elevate the risk for violence. Reducing these risk factors helps prevent violence, just like reducing risk factors for cancer helps prevent the disease. Not everyone who is obese or who smokes will get cancer, but obesity and smoking raise the risk for it. The clearest risk factor for gun violence is access to firearms. Having a gun does not cause gun violence, but gun violence would not occur without one. A gun in the home raises the likelihood of gun suicides and unintentional shootings and can make domestic violence more lethal.

Beyond access to firearms, research has identified individual, family, and community risk factors for violence generally. Prior violent behavior may be the strongest predictor of future violent behavior. In 2021 Nikolas Cruz pleaded guilty to seventeen counts of first-degree murder for a shooting at Marjory Stoneman Douglas High School in Parkland, Florida. Witnesses testified at his sentencing that Cruz had behaved violently since preschool. He hit other children, poisoned animals, and destroyed TVs and walls with baseball bats and his fists. Sheriff's deputies had been called to the Cruz house dozens of times from 2012 to 2016 to deal with violent outbursts. Research studies consistently find that people who have a history of violence commit violence at higher rates.

Severe mental health disorders—including depression, schizophrenia, and bipolar disorder—can also increase the risk of committing violence, particularly suicide. But the vast majority of people with a mental health disorder do not use a gun to harm themselves or anyone else. Other individual risk factors for violence include substance abuse, exposure to violent media, poor school achievement, and peer rejection.

Family and community factors also matter. Trauma is not only an outcome of violence but also a risk factor for it. Growing up in a family that struggles with substance abuse, child maltreatment, domestic violence, or exposure to community violence raises the chances of later committing violence. Trauma can change the brain, and children witnessing or experiencing violence can (but do not necessarily) become aggressive in response. Like trauma, poverty is both an outcome and a risk factor for violence. Racism and chronic underinvestment have impoverished some urban communities, leaving them without adequate jobs, stable housing, social services, and positive recreational outlets that otherwise support healthy development. "Concentrated poverty puts individuals, families, and communities under intense and unrelenting pressure," says crime researcher Thomas Abt. "When it persists over long periods, it leads to criminality and violence."[11] Communities with high crime rates also present more opportunities for residents to become involved in crime, which can lead to shootings.

No single factor explains why people shoot themselves or someone else. Different people facing the same difficult circumstances will not necessarily behave the same. Protective factors are things that buffer the hardships that might otherwise lead to violence. They include higher educational achievement and aspirations, close relationships with parents or other adults, healthy peer relationships, and participating in positive social activities.

The problem of gun violence is complex and impacts different groups of people differently. Solutions will need to address its multiple forms, consequences, and risk factors. Legislative and law enforcement solutions focus on limiting access to guns. Other solutions try to reduce the risk factors or increase the protective factors for violence.

CHAPTER TWO

Limit Access to Guns Through Additional Legislation

On May 25, 2022, Texas governor Greg Abbott spoke at a news conference that was consumed with grief and boiling with anger. The day before, a gunman had killed nineteen children and two teachers at Robb Elementary School in Uvalde, Texas. At the news conference, Abbott spoke about a mental health crisis in the area. He dismissed a call to implement stricter gun laws. New gun laws are not a "real solution" to gun violence, Abbott seethed. "There are more people who were shot every weekend in Chicago than there are in schools in Texas. . . . People who think that 'well maybe if we could just implement tougher gun laws, it's going to solve it. Chicago and LA and New York disprove that thesis."[12] The governors of California and Illinois, states known for strict gun laws, cried foul. Illinois governor J.B. Pritzker tweeted at Abbott, "You are lying about Chicago and what actually perpetuates gun violence. The majority of guns used in Chicago shootings come from states with lax gun laws. Do better."[13]

Gun laws spark intense political fights, but most people agree more can be done legislatively to reduce gun violence. In a 2022 Associated Press/NORC survey, 71 percent of

Americans said they want stricter gun laws. Sometimes even politicians agree with each other. In the summer of 2022, Congress passed the Bipartisan Safer Communities Act, the first piece of federal gun legislation in decades.

RAND, a nonpartisan research institute, believes Americans have similar values about reducing gun violence but lack facts about what laws work best. RAND's Gun Policy in America initiative attempts to fill the void. RAND's researchers analyzed more than twenty years of research that uses differences across states and time to identify the effectiveness of various gun laws. Based on the available evidence, RAND identified promising laws in three categories: laws that regulate who can own a gun, laws that regulate gun purchases, and laws that regulate gun storage and use. States with stronger gun laws have lower rates of gun violence, but some laws appear more effective than others at reducing violence.

Laws Limiting Who Owns a Gun

When news of the Uvalde shooting broke, Democratic senator Chris Murphy was presiding over the Senate chamber. Almost a decade earlier, Murphy had dedicated himself to the issue of gun safety after witnessing the aftermath of a school shooting in his home state of Connecticut. Twenty-seven people, including twenty children, died in the Sandy Hook Elementary School shooting in 2012. Ten years later, Murphy's pain was still evident. Moving to the Senate floor, his voice choked with regret for what Congress had not accomplished. "[I] beg my [Republican] colleagues. . . . Work with us to find a way to pass laws that make this less likely. . . . There is a common denominator that we can find. There is a place where we can achieve agreement."[14] The American public has already found one "common denominator." Many gun owners agree with non-owners

> "[I] beg my [Republican] colleagues. . . . Work with us to find a way to pass laws that make this less likely. . . . There is a common denominator that we can find. There is a place where we can achieve agreement."[14]
>
> —Chris Murphy, Democratic senator

Photos of the children killed by a gunman in Uvalde, Texas, in 2022 are displayed at this memorial in Austin, the state capital.

that certain people should not have access to firearms. More than 80 percent of Americans support laws that ban people convicted of domestic abuse from owning a gun. More than 75 percent support laws known as red flag laws that allow courts to temporarily remove a gun from a person at risk of violence.

Since 1968 federal law has prohibited people convicted of a felony, including a domestic violence felony, from buying or possessing a gun. More-recent federal legislation has also banned intimate partners convicted of a domestic violence misdemeanor and in some cases intimate partners with a domestic violence restraining order from gun ownership. State laws vary, including in how they define an intimate partner. Current and former spouses qualify, but some laws do not apply to dating partners who have not lived together. Dating partners commit more than half of intimate partner homicides, according to the Giffords Law Center. Federal legislation passed in 2022 extended some domestic violence bans to dating partners, but it does not stop dating partners with a restraining order from having a gun. Evidence suggests it should. Professor of criminal justice April Zeoli and colleagues found that when state bans for domestic violence restraining orders also applied to dating partners, intimate partner homicide rates dropped by 13 percent. Laws that deny guns to domestic abusers receive public support, and extending them could further reduce gun homicide.

Other laws restricting who can own a gun receive less support. RAND found some evidence that laws raising the minimum age to purchase a gun lower gun suicide rates. The relationship between age requirements and gun homicides generally or mass shootings specifically is inconclusive. Red flag laws receive considerable public support, and the 2022 federal gun legislation gives states money to implement them. However, RAND has not identified any rigorous studies that examine the impact of red flag laws on gun homicides. Their impact on gun suicides is uncertain. A lack of research evidence does not mean red flag laws cannot work, only that the connection has not been well studied.

Laws Regulating Gun Sales or Transfers

On May 24, 2022, while Murphy railed against his colleagues for lack of action, the coach of the Golden State Warriors basketball team did the same. Agitated and angry, Steve Kerr lashed out during a news conference. He pointed out that US senators refuse to pass universal background checks despite nearly all Americans supporting them. "It's pathetic,"[15] he said. Indeed, poll after poll finds that almost 90 percent of Americans support background checks for all purchases. Background checks restrict who can buy or be gifted a gun.

Since the 1990s, federal law has required licensed gun dealers to conduct background checks on customers seeking to buy a gun. Background checks compare information provided by purchasers to Federal Bureau of Investigation (FBI) records. Checks identify people who are prohibited from owning a gun, like convicted felons. In June 2022 background check requirements were extended to other commercial sellers but were not made universal. Although some states have universal background checks, federal law does not require one for private sales or transfers. That loop-

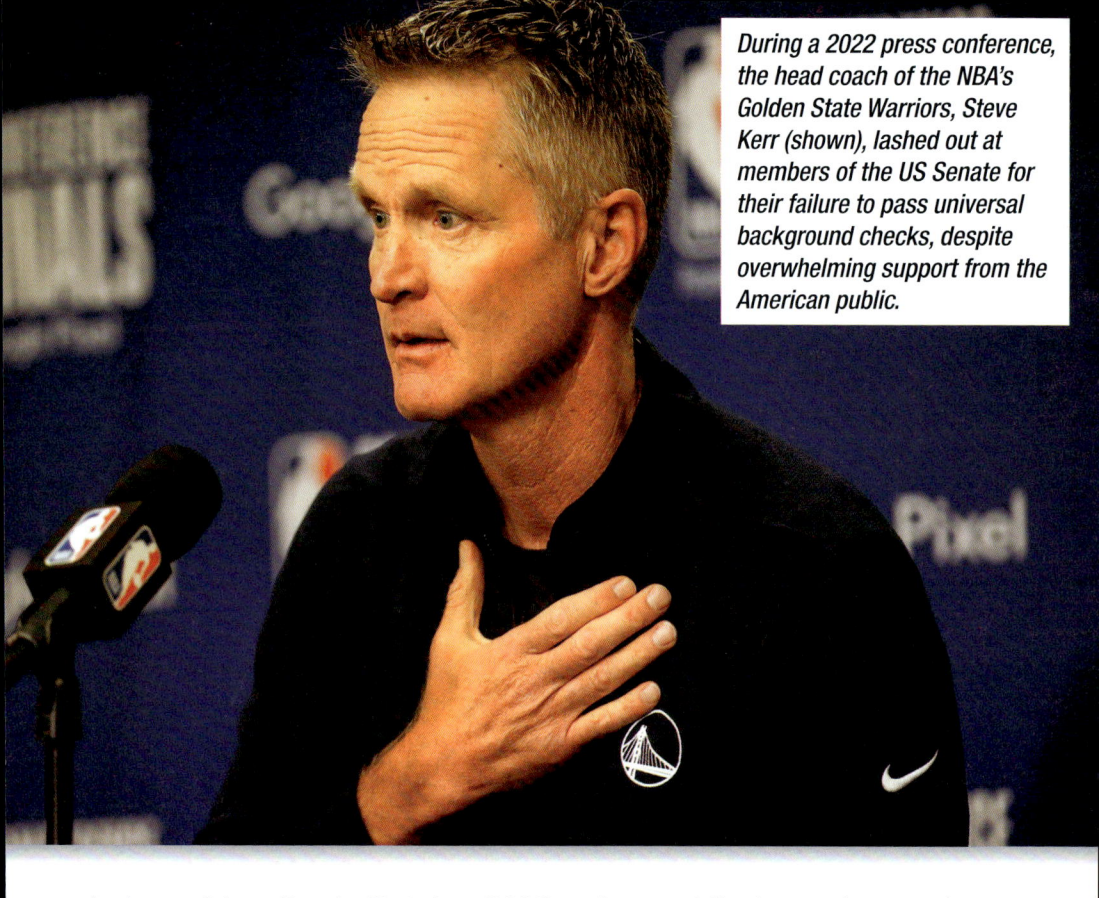

During a 2022 press conference, the head coach of the NBA's Golden State Warriors, Steve Kerr (shown), lashed out at members of the US Senate for their failure to pass universal background checks, despite overwhelming support from the American public.

hole could matter. In October 2022 a shooter killed a student and teacher at a St. Louis high school. The shooter, CNN reported, had tried to purchase a gun at a licensed dealer but failed a background check. He then purchased the AR-15-style rifle used in the shooting from a private seller. A universal background check law might have prevented him from obtaining the gun, but RAND finds evidence on extending background checks to private sales inconclusive. However, dealer background checks do correspond to lower rates of gun homicide, according to RAND.

Most background checks are completed in just a few minutes. Nine states have waiting periods, for at least some purchases, that require purchasers to wait before taking possession of a gun. Waiting periods vary from three to fourteen days. These laws try to prevent impulsive acts of violence, both self-inflicted and interpersonal. Waiting periods also give law enforcement more time to investigate a buyer's background, if needed. Gun rights activists argue that waiting periods infringe on a person's

The Missing Research

When RAND researchers undertook a massive effort to review the impact of gun laws on different forms of gun violence, they found a glaring lack of data. That is no surprise. The Dickey Amendment, which Congress passed in 1996, effectively shut down federal funding for gun research. When funding dried up, many researchers left the field. New researchers stopped entering it. Without facts, policy makers have had to rely heavily on conjecture and opinions. In 2019, after more than two decades, Congress rebooted funding for gun research, but research takes time. It also takes data, which are still missing. It is illegal for federal law enforcement to share gun trace data (which show where a gun used in a crime comes from) with researchers. There is no national registry of gun purchases, and data on gun injuries are incomplete. Without data, researchers struggle to answer questions such as these: How many people prohibited from owning a gun actually possess one? How do criminals get guns? What are the true consequences of gun violence? And, what is the impact of gun laws?

Second Amendment rights. "The big concern we have is when people want to exercise their right to bear arms, . . . they're delayed in their ability to get the tools that they need to protect themselves,"[16] says Sam Paredes, director of Gun Owners of California. RAND did not identify studies investigating the link between waiting periods and self-defense. But evidence shows that the laws correspond to decreases in gun suicides and homicides.

Permit-to-purchase and licensing laws are like waiting periods because they require purchasers to take an extra step before buying a gun. Such laws typically require a person to apply at a law enforcement agency in person for permission to purchase a gun. Like universal background checks, permit-to-purchase laws apply to purchases from both licensed dealers and private sellers. RAND found some evidence that permit or licensing requirements decrease firearm suicides among adults. One recent study led by public health researcher Daniel Webster suggests licensing laws also reduce fatal mass shootings.

Gun safety advocates promote bans on the sale of so-called assault weapons like the AR-15 rifle, but there is no consistent evidence linking such bans to reductions in gun violence, according to RAND. Most gun crimes involve handguns, not assault weapons, and most Republicans oppose assault-weapons bans, according to a 2022 Associated Press/NORC survey. Laws restricting gun purchases receive less support than laws restricting gun purchasers, but background checks, waiting periods, and permit-to-purchase laws appear to work.

Laws Controlling the Storage, Carrying, or Use of Guns

About 80 percent of gun purchases are made by people who already own a gun, according to researchers at Harvard and Northeastern Universities. Laws that control the storage or use of guns apply to all guns, not just new purchases. A substantial body of evidence suggests that adopting child-access-prevention laws and repealing stand-your-ground laws could reduce gun injuries and deaths.

Laws requiring safe gun storage may have prevented the 2021 death of DaMya Hudnall. DaMya loved to dance. She bounced down school hallways and across TikTok videos, the *Washington Post* reports. She was "full of awesome sauce,"[17] her mother says. But before DaMya even made it to high school, a gunshot extinguished her smile and infectious humor. In June 2021 a toddler unintentionally shot and killed the thirteen-year-old as she played a video game at home. A family friend had left the gun on top of the refrigerator next to cereal boxes and fruit snacks. If the gun had been safely stored, DaMya might be here today.

Child-access-prevention laws allow prosecutors to criminally charge adults who leave guns unattended and accessible to children. The laws motivate caregivers to secure guns with locks or in safes. Hiding a gun from a child is not enough. A study in rural Alabama found that 39 percent of parents who said their child did not know where they stored their guns were wrong. Children said they knew. Twenty-two percent of parents who claimed their child had never handled a gun in the household were also wrong. While many gun owners practice safe storage, some owners reject laws requiring it. They say such laws interfere with self-defense. RAND did not find research investigating the link between child-access-prevention laws and self-defense. But RAND found substantial evidence that child-access-prevention laws decrease self-inflicted gun injuries, suicides, and unintentional gun injuries and deaths.

Stand-your-ground laws allow the use of lethal force against an attacker if a person reasonably fears an attack could lead to death or serious injury. Unlike traditional self-defense laws, a person is not required to retreat even if it is possible. Thirty states have stand-your-ground laws. Supporters say they are important for self-defense and deter interpersonal gun violence. Critics say the laws escalate heated situations into deadly ones. The evidence shows that stand-your-ground laws are linked to gun homicides. A study of Florida, the first stand-your-ground state, found gun homicides increased by 32 percent after adopting the law.

Experts also say the application of the law is racially biased. Whether a shooter can claim self-defense under a stand-your-ground law depends on whether the shooter reasonably believed he or she was being seriously threatened. "The concept of 'reasonable fear' is anything but value-neutral," says Harvard University researcher Caroline Light. "Courtrooms are filled with people—judges, jurors, lawyers and witnesses—whose perceptions are shaped by the prejudices and implicit biases of our culture."[18] Research shows that when White shooters kill Black victims, shootings are ruled to be justified more often than when Black shooters kill White victims. Child-access-prevention laws and repealing stand-your-ground laws receive the strongest support out of all the laws RAND examined for reducing gun violence.

> "The concept of 'reasonable fear' is anything but value-neutral. Courtrooms are filled with people—judges, jurors, lawyers and witnesses—whose perceptions are shaped by the prejudices and implicit biases of our culture."[18]
>
> — Caroline Light, Harvard University researcher

Pros and Cons of New Gun Legislation

Gun laws can work. RAND's review of the data finds some support for minimum age requirements and permit-to-purchase laws. It finds moderate evidence for background checks, waiting peri-

Arming Teachers

After any school shooting, cries to arm teachers erupt on conservative news and social media. The best thing to stop a bad guy with a gun is a good guy with a gun, they say. But is it? No research has investigated the impact of arming teachers. Some teachers and parents take comfort in the idea that a school shooter might immediately meet armed resistance. But over 75 percent of prekindergarten through grade 12 teachers do not want teachers to be armed, according to a 2022 survey by the American Federation of Teachers. They believe that arming teachers would make schools less safe. The Giffords Law Center identified over one hundred examples of adults mishandling guns in schools during the period from 2014 to 2021. Many incidents involved adults leaving guns unattended, often in a restroom. Other incidents involved unintentional shootings or adults threatening someone with a gun. Also, effectively using a gun during a crisis requires more than just being a good shot. Police and soldiers typically have extensive training to deal with the fear, confusion, and stress of crisis situations. Despite the problems, over half of states allow school staff other than security guards to carry a gun.

ods, and prohibitions for domestic violence offenders. The review found substantial evidence for child-access-prevention laws and repealing stand-your-ground laws. Different laws address different forms of violence, but altogether, extending these laws in scope or geography may reduce self-inflicted, interpersonal, and unintentional gun injuries and deaths. Many Americans say they support them, and although rare, political compromises can happen, as Congress demonstrated in 2022. When laws are adopted and enforced, they can have an immediate impact.

But enacting new gun laws is controversial and difficult. Even though most Americans say they want stricter gun laws, they often disagree on the details. Politicians are even more divided, even in the face of tragedies like the Uvalde, Texas, school shooting. The effectiveness of new laws also depends in part on how easily they can be evaded. Adopting stricter gun laws makes less difference in areas where illegal guns can be easily obtained. The effectiveness of gun laws also depends on whether police and courts actually enforce them.

CHAPTER THREE

Improve the Enforcement of Gun Laws

Shanae Clayton tried to escape her abuser. The stresses and isolation of the COVID-19 pandemic had aggravated an already bad situation. Her boyfriend had lost his job. He had started drinking more, and the violence escalated. After recovering from a severe bout with the coronavirus, Clayton decided life was too short to stay in a bad relationship. But before she could leave, Clayton's boyfriend shot and killed her. He should never even have had a gun. He was a convicted felon. All states and the federal government ban felons from owning firearms. "It's absolutely outrageous that we're losing people in this way, because we know what we need to do in order to prevent it from happening. We have laws on the books. We're just not enforcing them,"[19] says law professor Natalie Nanasi.

Having laws is not enough. Curbing gun violence will require better law enforcement. Experts agree that disarming prohibited possessors; using red flag laws; strengthening the Bureau of Alcohol, Tobacco, Firearms and Explosives (ATF); and improving the relationship between police and underserved communities could help reduce gun injuries and deaths.

26

Disarm Prohibited Possessors

Federal law prohibits certain people from owning a gun, including convicted felons, domestic violence offenders, illegal drug users, people ruled mentally incompetent, and anyone dishonorably discharged from the military. Despite federal and state laws, many people who have been disqualified from owning a gun still have one. The number of such owners is unclear. There is no national registry of gun owners. California, however, has a state registry. In 2021 it showed that almost twenty-four thousand people banned from owning a gun had one. Disarming prohibited possessors could reduce gun violence. The Washington State Coalition Against Domestic Violence estimated that more than half of domestic violence gun homicides in 2014 were committed by people banned from owning a gun. Everytown, an advocacy group, estimates that one-third of mass shootings have been perpetrated by prohibited possessors.

> "It's absolutely outrageous that we're losing people in this way, because we know what we need to do in order to prevent it from happening. We have laws on the books. We're just not enforcing them."[19]
>
> —Natalie Nanasi, law professor

Law enforcement agencies encounter multiple problems in removing guns from disqualified owners. Only a handful of states specify how such people should turn in their guns after a ban—for example, following a felony conviction. Poor law enforcement coordination and limited resources also explain why guns end up in the wrong hands. Some local authorities fail to update information in the federal background check system. Without accurate records, background checks will not stop prohibited possessors from buying a gun. Removing a banned weapon also takes time and effort. Police must determine whether a person suspected of illegally possessing a gun actually has one, then strategize how to remove a prohibited gun from a potentially dangerous and angry person. When California set up a task force to remove guns from prohibited possessors, it took one team of agents nine hours to visit six locations and ultimately remove just two guns, according

> "You can't just ask an over-whelmed police department to [confiscate illegal guns] in their spare time."[20]
>
> —Dan Satterberg, King County, Washington, prosecutor

to CBS News. "You can't just ask an over-whelmed police department to do this in their spare time,"[20] says King County, Washington, prosecutor Dan Satterberg. Disarming prohibited possessors is a time-consuming, resource-intensive, and dangerous job.

The King County Regional Domestic Violence Enforcement Unit in Washington has succeeded where other departments have failed. Created in 2018, the unit has police, sheriff's deputies, prosecutors, victim advocates, and court liaisons who specialize in removing guns from domestic abusers. They work across jurisdictions, prioritizing the highest-risk cases. They interview victims to learn what guns their abusers possess and then send a special unit to retrieve the firearms. In 2016, before the program started, the county collected just 124 guns. In 2018 the specialized unit collected more than 466 guns, according to Safer Families, Safer Communities. Enforcing laws that ban dangerous people from owning guns depends on adequate resources and coordination.

A clerk in a gun shop in Milford, Michigan, checks a customer's paperwork for a background check before completing the sale of a firearm.

Second Amendment Sanctuaries

Lax law enforcement is sometimes a choice. Second Amendment sanctuaries are counties or states that refuse to enforce gun laws that they say infringe on people's constitutional right to bear arms. Over one thousand communities and seventeen states are Second Amendment sanctuaries, according to gun-related news outlet the Trace. After Colorado passed a red flag law in 2019, at least thirty-seven counties adopted sanctuary resolutions. Some sheriffs believe the red flag law violates individuals' right to due process. Weld County sheriff Steve Reams told a CBS News reporter, "There are portions of the law I just flat out can't and won't do." Most Second Amendment sanctuary resolutions withhold resources to enforce gun laws that the sanctuary county or state deems unconstitutional. The state of Missouri goes much further. Its Second Amendment Preservation Act allows citizens to sue for $50,000 if they think a local government or police agency violated their gun rights. Ultimately, courts will decide whether states and counties can refuse to implement federal laws. In the meantime, thinking has evolved in some sanctuaries. Two and a half years after Colorado's red flag law passed, twenty of the thirty-seven sanctuary counties had used it.

Quoted in CBS News, "Several Colorado Sheriffs Say They Won't Enforce Red Flag Gun Law," November 15, 2019. www.cbsnews.com.

Use Red Flag Laws More Often

In May 2022 Payton Gendron killed ten people in a racist attack at Tops supermarket in Buffalo, New York. The teenager had come to the attention of police before the mass shooting. In the prior year, Gendron had told teachers he planned to commit a murder-suicide. The teen later told school staff he was joking, but the school alerted authorities. Gendron was taken for a psychological evaluation, but police did nothing to limit his access to firearms. Some say they could have.

New York, like eighteen other states, allows for extreme risk protection orders, known as red flag laws. These laws authorize courts to temporarily ban access to guns for people deemed at high risk of violence. In all red flag states, law enforcement can petition courts for protection orders to remove guns. In some states family members, doctors, and school administrators can

Mourners attend a vigil outside the Tops supermarket that was the scene of a mass shooting in Buffalo, New York, in 2022. Although New York has a law that allows authorities to temporarily ban access to guns for people deemed at high risk of violence, gun safety advocates say that the law was not properly implemented.

also petition. Referring to the Buffalo shooting, Christian Heyne, a gun safety advocate at Brady: United Against Gun Violence, said, "This is the kind of story that these [protection] orders have been created for. . . . The tool wasn't implemented the way that New York designed."[21]

Gun safety advocates believe red flag laws will reduce gun violence—and Congress recently allocated money to help states implement the laws. But researchers at RAND find little evidence that red flag laws work. That may be because red flag laws are so rarely used. "It's as if the law doesn't exist,"[22] says sociologist Jeffrey Swanson. In Chicago, for example, the Associated Press reported only four uses of red flag laws over a period in which eighteen hundred gun deaths occurred. Often the public, and sometimes even police, are unaware of the laws. People who know about the laws can struggle with the process of petitioning courts. Some localities have teams that help file extreme risk protection orders, and several states have recently allocated funds for training. Greater awareness of red flag laws may make them more effective.

Enable the ATF to Better Enforce Laws

A lack of data makes it impossible to get an accurate breakdown of where guns used in crimes come from. But experts agree that many, perhaps most, guns used to commit crimes are illegally acquired. Some are stolen. Others come directly or indirectly from a small number of licensed gun dealers. A so-called straw purchase occurs when someone who can legally buy a gun purchases one on behalf of a disqualified buyer. Gun traffickers buy multiple guns from a licensed dealer and then sell them on the streets. It is generally illegal to buy a gun from a dealer for someone else because a dealer must run a background check on the actual owner. Gun dealers can identify illegal purchases by noticing suspicious behavior. Does a customer select a gun yet his or her companion completes the background check? Does a companion hand cash to a purchaser inside or just outside of the store? Does a customer buy several guns within a short time or purchase duplicates?

Almost all licensed gun dealers follow the rules. But some unethical dealers knowingly sell guns directly to felons and other prohibited possessors. Five percent of dealers supply 90 percent of guns used in crimes, according to Brady: United Against Gun Violence. In 2021 the city of Chicago filed a lawsuit against Westforth Sports, a northwest Indiana gun shop located just across the Illinois-Indiana border from Chicago. According to the Chicago Police Department, one in every five guns used in a crime and recovered in Chicago comes from Indiana, a state with laxer gun laws than Illinois. The city of Chicago alleges that Westforth sold guns to obvious straw purchasers and gun traffickers like Kadeem Fryer, who purchased thirteen guns within thirty days, including many duplicates.

The ATF is the federal law enforcement agency that regulates gun dealers. It cited Westforth Sports thirty-nine times, and inspectors twice recommended revoking its firearms license, according to the legal complaint filed by Chicago. But Westforth still operates today. It is not an unusual story. The ATF inspects about ten thousand of approximately eighty thousand gun dealers a year. An investigation by the Trace and *USA Today* showed that even with abundant evidence, the ATF rarely revokes a license.

Some gun rights advocates believe a strong ATF threatens their interests and have lobbied Congress accordingly. Congress has restricted the ATF's power by limiting the frequency of inspections, setting an unusually high bar for revoking licenses, and underfunding the agency. While president, Barack Obama told a town hall, "One of the most frustrating things that I hear is when people say—who are opposed to any further laws, why don't you just enforce the laws that are on the books, and those very same members of Congress then cut ATF budgets to make it impossible to enforce the law."[23] Slowing the supply of guns used in crimes by enforcing current laws could reduce gun violence, but it requires political will. In the meantime, Chicago, other cities, and even victims are trying to force change through the courts.

Build Trust Between Police and Underserved Communities

Sometimes the problem with law enforcement is not inaction but unjust action. Actual and perceived police misconduct damages public trust. Without trust, people hesitate to report crimes, and gun violence can go unchecked. Research led by sociologist Matthew Desmond and published in 2016 shows how police brutality can suppress crime reporting. In 2004, according to federal court documents, Milwaukee police officers viciously assaulted Frank Jude Jr., an unarmed Black man. Three former officers were later sentenced to more than fifteen years in federal prison for their roles in the attack. Researchers tracked weekly 911 calls before and after the *Milwaukee Journal Sentinel* reported the attack. Crime reports to 911 dropped significantly after the news broke, especially in Milwaukee's Black neighborhoods. One year later, the number of calls had still not rebounded. The

Using Civil Law to Reform the Gun Industry

Frustrated with the ATF's lack of enforcement, some gun violence victims and safety advocates have turned to civil courts. Lawsuits can shape public opinion and motivate businesses to change their practices, as decades of litigation did in the tobacco industry. The gun industry poses a bigger challenge. The federal government and states have given the industry multiple immunity protections. Still, some lawsuits have succeeded. Joshua Higbee died in a mass shooting at a factory in Hesston, Kansas, in 2016. The legal complaint alleged that the shooter's AK-47 semiautomatic rifle and Glock semiautomatic pistol came from a straw purchase made at a pawn shop. The family sued, and the store closed after settling the lawsuit in 2018 with the Higbee family and other victims for $2 million. Victims of other mass shootings are using a similar strategy. In 2022 three families of people killed in a shooting at a July 4 parade sued the online gun shops that sold the weapons to the alleged shooter.

researchers estimate that twenty-two thousand calls were never made. It is not just egregious police conduct that harms the relationship between police and residents. When people feel like police have treated them unfairly in everyday encounters or when police repeatedly fail to solve crimes, police legitimacy erodes over time. Legitimacy and effectiveness are closely linked. As crime researcher Thomas Abt says, "Legitimacy deficits create a catch-22: to improve safety, there must be trust, but to improve trust, there must be safety."[24] In all communities, residents want police to solve crimes, but good law enforcement requires a healthy relationship between the police and residents.

Procedural justice is a promising approach to improve policing. It focuses on the interactions between police and residents, not just the outcomes. Procedural justice has four elements. Interactions should be respectful. Everyone should have an opportunity to share their perspective. Police should explain their decisions, and decisions should be fair. In a guide for police, public safety researchers Laura Kunard and Charlene Moe detail

> "Legitimacy deficits create a catch-22: to improve safety, there must be trust, but to improve trust, there must be safety."[24]
>
> —Thomas Abt, crime researcher

examples of procedural justice. They tell the story of a state trooper who accompanied the Springfield, Massachusetts, SWAT team to raid a suspected drug house. Despite the chaotic scene, the trooper took the time to explain to neighbors what was happening. In another example, when a local park became a hot spot for violence in Sioux Falls, South Dakota, the police explained neighbors' concerns to the people involved, then listened to their concerns. Following the meeting, the city made improvements to the park that helped resolve the problem. Procedural justice can build trust over time by showing residents that police respect community members and want to work together.

Procedural justice techniques can be learned, and such training has payoffs. A procedural justice approach improves resi-

At a 2016 live town hall event with CNN's Anderson Cooper, President Barack Obama expressed frustration that members of Congress advocate stricter enforcement of existing gun laws while at the same time cutting the budget of the agency responsible for enforcement of those laws.

dents' perceptions of police and is linked to better community cooperation. Research has not proved a link to gun violence reduction, but some experts feel confident it exists. Procedural justice alone cannot reduce gun violence. Unjust officers must also be held accountable for their actions, and underserved communities require money and resources to fight crime.

Pros and Cons of Improving Law Enforcement

Republicans and Democrats say they agree that having gun laws is not enough and that reducing gun violence requires better enforcement. More resources and better coordination would help police disarm prohibited possessors at higher rates and also enable the ATF to hold more gun dealers accountable. Training could encourage wider use of red flag laws and build trust between police and communities. Improved law enforcement can curb gun violence.

Despite what both sides say, however, moves to improve law enforcement is politically divisive. Law enforcement can be as controversial as new legislation. Increasing law enforcement also requires time, money, and staff that are often hard to find. Some people say it is time to focus on solutions outside of the legal system.

CHAPTER FOUR

Implement Programs Targeting High-Risk Individuals

Miayon Medley had eluded Jamal West for months. The middle-aged West could not keep up with the fast-footed teen weaving through the streets of Baltimore. But West was relentless. That is part of West's job as an outreach worker for Roca, an organization helping youth involved in dangerous or criminal behavior. When West finally caught up to Medley, the teen made it clear that he did not want the help. Soon after, Medley landed in a coma when he injured himself trying to outrun police. Even after he woke up from the coma, Medley had a long recovery. For two months, Medley's grandmother visited him in the hospital, and so did West. Eventually West's persistence paid off. Medley accepted help. Roca gave him therapy, job training, and assistance finding employment. Medley worked hard to change his life, and in 2021 Roca honored him with an award for his achievements.

Traditionally, the legal system has been the main tool to solve gun violence. Programs like Roca use a public health approach instead. They focus on prevention and address the underlying causes of violence. Only a small number of people are at risk of becoming shooters. Identifying them and changing their behaviors can make communities and organizations safer. Violence interruption programs operate in urban neighborhoods suffering from concentrated poverty and high levels of crime. Behavioral threat assessment programs operate in workplaces and schools to prevent mass shootings. In both cases, programs identify at-risk individuals and provide supports and deterrents to change their behavior.

Community Violence Interruption Programs

In all communities, including urban communities suffering from high rates of crime, most people are law abiding and peaceful. Sociologist Andrew Papachristos has found that only a few hundred people out of tens of thousands are involved in urban gun violence. Even within gangs, crime researcher Thomas Abt found that only a few members typically use guns. Despite their small numbers, individuals involved in gun violence put entire communities at risk of physical and mental harm. Their actions instill fear, perpetuate trauma, and lead to the spread of violence. Before creating the Cure Violence program, Dr. Gary Slutkin spent a decade fighting diseases like cholera and AIDS in Africa. He likens American gun violence to an epidemic and prescribes a public health approach to end it. "There's a way to reverse epidemics," says Slutkin. "The first of it is interrupting transmission. In order to interrupt transmission you need to detect and find first cases."[25] First cases are the people responsible for the spread of a disease. Violence intervention programs attempt to change the behavior of specific people at the center of the problem to prevent violence from spreading.

Programs differ in the details but use a similar strategy. They identify who is most at risk of involvement in violence, build relationships with these individuals, intervene in crisis situations, connect individuals to support services, and generally promote peace. Hospital-based intervention programs like Caught in the

Crossfire approach gun violence victims in emergency rooms to interrupt any plans for retaliation. Other programs rely on staff's local knowledge, crime data, and police to identify people to recruit into their programs. Some programs approach groups known to be at the center of violence, while other programs recruit one person at a time.

Street outreach workers, also known as violence interrupters, are the programs' frontline workers. Outreach workers build trust with recruits over months and years. They walk the neighborhoods and check in frequently with program participants. Some outreach workers were once involved in violence themselves. Their personal histories and knowledge of who and what drives violence in their communities gives them credibility. "These coaches . . . [have] been there before and they are guiding us. . . . They have genuine love for us. We've got someone in our corner that is real,"[26] says Damien, a participant in Chicago CRED. Outreach workers show up to crisis situations anywhere, anytime, to deescalate conflicts.

Outreach workers for a violence intervention program walk their Brooklyn, New York, neighborhood. Known as "violence Interrupters," outreach workers attempt to identify individuals most at risk of involvement in violence and promote peace.

They monitor developing situations and connect recruits with services such as therapy, job training, education, housing, and health care.

Programs leverage the existing strengths of communities and collaborate with other organizations to provide services. Some programs like Operation Ceasefire involve police, while others, like Cure Violence, do not. But even when police are involved, it is as part of a community team. David Kennedy, who helped develop Boston's Operation Ceasefire, believes policing is not the best lever for change. "The most powerful influencer of behavior is not the cops—it's what you and your community and your mom and your best friends and your girlfriend think about what you're doing,"[27] he says.

> "The most powerful influencer of behavior is not the cops—it's what you and your community and your mom and your best friends and your girlfriend think about what you're doing."[27]
>
> —David Kennedy, developer of Boston's Operation Ceasefire

The Impact of Community Violence Interruption Programs

Research shows violence intervention programs can work. Neighborhoods in Chicago, New York, Philadelphia, Boston, and Baltimore experienced reductions in shootings, gun injuries, or gun homicides after adopting such programs. For example, the Cure Violence program in the South Bronx area of New York City was associated with a significant reduction (46 percentage points) in shootings per year than a similar community without the program, according to researchers from New York's John Jay College of Criminal Justice. But these programs do not always work. The same study found no reduction in shootings at a second New York City location. Lack of funding or community buy-in, problems finding or keeping staff, and poor communication with partner organizations make it difficult for programs to operate consistently. Consistency is critical for building trust with recruits. Other programs have faltered when social services are not readily available to offer participants.

Although violence intervention programs have existed for decades, interest in them has surged. Calls for defunding the police

Violence Interrupter: A Hazardous Job

Violence interrupters are frontline workers in the public health approach to solving gun violence. Typically working in high-crime, low-income urban communities, violence interrupters break up disputes, disrupt cycles of violence, and help spread peace. It is a dangerous job. In a 2021 survey of Chicago outreach workers, sociologist Andrew Papachristos and colleagues found that one-third of workers reported witnessing someone being shot while on the job. One-fifth reported being shot at themselves. Many violence interrupters themselves have experienced violence and run-ins with the law in the past. Experiencing trauma on the job takes a mental toll directly and can cause workers to relive past trauma. Violence interrupters receive low pay, few job benefits, little training, and limited opportunities for advancement. Inconsistent program funding makes for unstable employment. These workers do the job because they care deeply about their communities, but having to endure such job conditions is, some believe, inconsistent with the importance of their work.

have directed attention to nonpolicing interventions. Chicago, Philadelphia, and Baltimore recently announced large funding increases for such programs, and in 2022 the federal Bipartisan Safer Communities Act allocated $250 million for them.

Behavioral Threat Assessment

Like violence intervention programs, behavioral threat assessment teams identify specific individuals at risk of committing violence and put them on a different path. Instead of focusing on community violence, threat assessment teams work specifically to prevent shootings in schools and workplaces. In the late 1990s the FBI published a profile of school shooters based on previous school shootings. The list suggested traits to help schools and police identify potential shooters. The traits included "seemed to have trouble with their parents," "listened to songs that promote violence," "appeared . . . sloppy or unkempt in dress," and "dislike[d] popular students or students who bully others."[28] Critics quickly pointed out the uselessness of those descriptors for identifying the next school shooter. They apply to a large number of teens, almost none of whom will ever commit an act of gun violence. "It is impossible to predict who will go on the next rampage by focusing on types of people,"[29] says journalist Mark Follman. Trying to identify a potential shooter based on traits does not work and threatens to unfairly stigmatize certain students.

> "What is so tragic about school shootings is that in virtually every case, somebody knew something that in retrospect was a warning sign."[30]
>
> —Peter Langman, expert on school shooters

Behavioral threat assessment instead uses patterns of behavior to identify potential shooters. Most mass shooters do not suddenly snap. Instead, they develop plans over time and often share those plans with others. "What is so tragic about school shootings is that in virtually every case, somebody knew something that in retrospect was a warning sign,"[30] says Peter Langman, an

Demeatreas Whatley, who works for Cure Violence, looks over an antiviolence sign in his office in Chicago in 2018. The Cure Violence program in New York City was associated with a 46 percent reduction in shootings per year than a similar community without the program.

expert on school shooters. The fact that shooters often discuss their plans is not just a tragedy. It is also an opportunity to prevent violence.

How Behavioral Threat Assessment Works

Follman is one person trying to understand what more can be done to prevent mass shootings. In 2019 he observed the threat assessment team in Oregon's Salem-Keizer School District. Follman attended the team's weekly meeting the day it discussed the case of a high school junior Follman calls Brandon. Fifteen members of the multidisciplinary team—with expertise in education, psychology, law enforcement, and social services—reviewed the case. The week before, a student overheard Brandon tell a classmate he was planning to bring his father's semiautomatic gun to school and shoot it up. The fellow student told a teacher, and the comment was quickly given to the threat assessment team. A school resource officer immediately followed up with Brandon and his mother at home. Brandon claimed his comment was a joke. With permission, the officer searched Brandon's room for weapons but did not find any. When Brandon returned to school two days later, school security stayed vigilant. Meanwhile, the assessment team investigated, interviewing students, teachers, Brandon, and his mother.

At the team's weekly meeting, members reviewed the findings, according to Follman. A concerning pattern of behavior emerged. Brandon had made similar comments about committing a school shooting twice before. Interviews revealed that Brandon had skipped classes recently, suffered a humiliation in drama club and quit, behaved aggressively toward a teacher, and acted depressed. When interviewed, Brandon said he had no friends. The specificity of Brandon's threat and the number of people raising concerns worried the team. But there was no evidence of attack planning or attempts to obtain a gun. In the end, the team rated Brandon a moderate risk for violence. Administrators increased supervision but also provided academic help and counseling. The

Anonymous Tip Lines and Threat Assessments

Behavioral threat assessment cannot work in a vacuum. It relies on tips about concerning behaviors. In 81 percent of school shootings, a shooter told someone about his or her thoughts or plans, according to the National Threat Assessment Center. Past shooters have made comments to classmates or teachers, on school assignments, or in social media posts. Anonymous reporting systems can help ensure that people who hear something feel comfortable saying something. Almost two-thirds of public schools have an anonymous tip line, according to the National Center for Education Statistics. Colorado's statewide system, Safe2Tell, allows students, staff, parents, and the community to make anonymous reports online, by mobile app, or over the phone. During the 2021–2022 school year, the tip line received over nineteen thousand reports. Fourteen percent related to suicide and 4 percent to weapons or a planned school attack. School climate also matters. In schools where students and staff have good communication and positive connections, students feel more comfortable reporting concerns. School shooters do not always share their plans, but developing a positive school climate and anonymous reporting help ensure that authorities can respond effectively when plans are shared.

team encouraged two teachers Brandon liked to make a special effort to reach out to him. Brandon was soon talking about plans to get a driver's license and a summer job. By fall he seemed happier, and he eventually graduated without incident. Whether the early intervention prevented violence will never be known. At a minimum, the threat assessment process brought help to someone who needed it.

Threat assessment teams find people in crisis and deter them from harming themselves or others. The National Threat Assessment Center, part of the US Secret Service, recommends that teams consist of people with varied expertise who meet regularly and use clearly defined guidelines about what behaviors are problematic and how to report them. Investigations should gather information about the motives and stressors driving the concerning behavior and also a student's capacity for carrying out violence. Does a student have a plan, have

Many teenage students experience stress and unhappiness during their school years, but students whose behavior raises concerns among teachers and staff may be referred to threat assessment teams.

access to weapons, or accept violence as a solution to problems? Teams examine a student's communications, including classwork and social media posts, and also assess a student's positive social connections. Using the gathered information, the team intervenes with appropriate support services or, if necessary, removes a student temporarily from school. Workplace threat assessment teams operate similarly.

Threat assessments do not alleviate the need for emergency response plans, but experts believe such efforts can help prevent gun violence. Evaluating whether they really work is difficult because mass shootings in workplaces and schools are rare. The absence of a shooting could mean the process succeeded or that the threat was not real. So researchers consider other measures of success. Studies have found that schools with a threat assessment process have a better school climate, fewer suspensions, more counseling, and less aggressive student behavior.

Pros and Cons of Intervention Programs

Violence intervention programs target specific individuals at the highest risk of committing violence and provide supports to reroute them toward healthier pathways. These programs can work to reduce gun violence. Because the programs focus resources where they may make the most difference, these programs can be relatively cost effective. Such interventions may be particularly important in communities that have low trust in police.

However, interventions targeting high-risk individuals do not always work. They depend not only on consistent financial support but also finding and retaining effective staff. Programs need to be coupled with social services such as counseling and job referral that provide help and incentives for change, but sometimes these services are not readily available. Also, addressing the underlying causes of violence takes time. Violence interrupters, for example, spend months working to build trust. For politicians under pressure to demonstrate results and communities dodging gunfire, the timeline for change can feel too long. Violence intervention programs cannot be the only solution, but they can be one part.

CHAPTER FIVE

Change the Environment to Change Behavior

In 2020, gun violence surpassed car accidents as the leading cause of death for American youth ages one to nineteen, according to CDC data. Americans spend hours every week in vehicles, but still, more youth now die from bullets. That alarming fact is not completely unexpected. Gun deaths among youth have been rising for the past decade. "The increasing firearm-related mortality reflects a longer-term trend and shows that we continue to fail to protect our youth from a preventable cause of death,"[31] write public health researchers from the University of Michigan.

The change in the leading cause of death for youth is not just a tragic story of rising gun violence. It is also a good-news story about declining car crash fatalities. In 1946, 9.35 Americans died per 100 million vehicle miles traveled. In 2020 just 1.34 did, according to the National Highway Traffic Safety Administration. Public health researchers David Hemenway and Matthew Miller attribute the steep decline to multiple efforts that began decades ago when health professionals started investigating the problem. Before then, solutions to car crash fatalities focused on changing the behavior of drivers. If drivers always obeyed the law and never made mistakes, car crashes would not occur. Public health professionals in the 1950s did not focus just on the behavior of

46

drivers. They discovered, according to Hemenway and Miller, that "many injuries occurred when the steering column impaled the driver's chest, . . . when passengers were thrown from the car, and when the car left the road and hit lampposts and trees that had been planted alongside the highway. Public health advocates started asking, Why can't the car be made safer, the roads safer . . . , the emergency medical system (EMS) better?"[32] Instead of changing the behavior of drivers, public health advocates worked to improve cars and roads. Over the following decades, seat belts, airbags, collapsible steering columns, and padded dashboards became standard. Speed bumps, guardrails, and median barriers became more common. Programs aimed at changing social norms—getting people to wear seatbelts and not drink and drive—helped change behavior. When combined with stricter laws, changing drivers' environments dramatically cut car crash fatalities.

> "The increasing firearm-related mortality reflects a longer-term trend and shows that we continue to fail to protect our youth from a preventable cause of death."[31]
>
> —Jason E. Goldstick, Rebecca Cunningham, and Patrick Carter, public health researchers

Could a similar approach reduce gun violence? Research shows interventions that invest in places and populations (rather than specific people) can work. These interventions change individuals' behavior indirectly by changing what shapes that behavior. Just like some individuals are at higher risk of gun violence, some places are too. Physically changing the environment can cool criminal hot spots. Bringing resources to underserved places and populations can address the underlying causes of violence. Johnny Page, director of a not-for-profit that helps communities heal from violence, thinks the approach makes sense. "When a flower doesn't bloom," he says, "you don't fix the flower, you fix the environment that it is growing in."[33]

Interventions That Change the Physical Environment

Some interventions reduce gun crime by changing the spaces where it occurs. Keith Green is the architect of one such effort. He grew up in a drab South Philadelphia neighborhood with concrete buildings and lacking green grass and trees. Every time Green left home, a blighted lot across the street confronted him. "Every day seeing a site that's full of trash, overgrown with weeds, the owner of record is nowhere to be found—you feel like you can't do anything,"[34] he says. Green knew neighborhoods did not have to look that way. When he visited his grandmother's house, Green spent hours tending her garden filled with colorful annuals and rose bushes. At first, the weeding, pruning, and planting was just the way his grandmother kept Green out of trouble. Eventually, Green chose gardening as a career. Today he directs a program at the Pennsylvania Horticultural Society that revitalizes vacant lots, like the one from his old neighborhood. The purpose of the program is to reduce community violence and improve mental health. When he started, Green did not believe it would work. He

Research suggests that the same kinds of interventions that reduced traffic deaths, such as seatbelt laws, might also help reduce gun violence. Instead of changing the behavior of drivers, public health advocates worked to improve car and road safety.

Changing Norms for Safer Gun Storage

Just like other aspects of an environment, norms influence individuals' behavior. Public service campaigns count on that influence, and when it comes to gun violence, the American Academy of Pediatrics does too. The academy urges pediatricians to talk to families about storing guns safely. Some people worry that the topic is too controversial for doctors to address. Pediatrician Dorothy R. Novick is not concerned. "We are used to having conversations about personal aspects of peoples' lives. When we approach safe storage collaboratively and without judgment, when we center the conversation around child safety and when we steer clear of politics, we find patients and families open and receptive," says Novick. Families trust their pediatricians, which makes their advice matter. Indeed, one study found that when pediatricians discuss storage with families and provide gun locks if requested, the rates of safe gun storage increase. Like the public health approach more generally, pediatricians attempt to reduce gun violence with facts, with prevention, and without judgment.

Dorothy R. Novick. "Opinion: 2020 Was the Worst Year Ever for Child Gun Deaths. We Need Prevention Strategies Now," *Washington Post*, June 21, 2021. www.washingtonpost.com.

soon realized that plants could transform more than just his life. They can transform whole communities.

In high-crime urban neighborhoods, violence concentrates in highly specific locations. These can be near bus stops, liquor stores, or abandoned houses. Sometimes a hot spot is a block or a vacant lot. Cities that have experienced significant population declines often teem with vacant lots. Philadelphia has an estimated forty thousand, according to the city. Detroit has an estimated 24 square miles (62 sq. km) of them. Filled with tall weeds, trash, old tires, and broken-down cars, the lots can become hiding places for guns, drugs, and criminal activity.

Cleaning and greening interventions turn vacant lots into pocket parks by cleaning up trash and weeds, planting grass and trees, and installing a low wooden fence. These lots, once a source of crime and fear, transform into spaces for playtime, football games, and barbecues. Multiple studies show that cleaning and greening works. Research led by epidemiologist

Multiple studies show that cleaning up vacant lots reduces violence by turning spaces that were once hiding places for criminal activity into locations for playtime, games, and barbecues.

Charles Branas found that one intervention in Philadelphia reduced gun violence by 29 percent in neighborhoods below the poverty line. Cleaning and greening are also cost effective. In another study, Branas and colleagues estimated that every dollar invested saved $26 to $333 in lost productivity and medical, police, and incarceration costs. Greening does not just reduce gun violence. It also makes people feel safer and improves mental health.

Similarly, refurbishing abandoned houses reduces gun assaults, according to a study led by health researcher Eugenia South. These interventions make neighborhoods safer by limiting opportunities for criminal activity. South suggests that they also work by changing thoughts and interactions. "Every time we step out of our houses the places and spaces around us are influencing us," says South. "They're influencing our physiology. They're influencing our state of mind, our thought processes, how we connect with people."[35] Well-tended spaces can improve mental health and foster positive connections among neighbors, which are protective factors against involvement in violence.

> "Every time we step out of our houses the places and spaces around us are influencing us. They're influencing our physiology. They're influencing our state of mind, our thought processes, how we connect with people."[35]
>
> —Eugenia South, health researcher

Other changes to the physical environment can similarly impact gun violence. Operation Cul-de-Sac, implemented by the Los Angeles Police Department in the 1990s, strategically placed concrete barriers on blocks known as hot spots to stop cars from driving through. Gun violence fell by 20 percent in one year, according to crime researcher James Lasley. Restricting the number of liquor stores or where and when alcohol is sold is also associated with decreases in violence. Interventions that change the physical environment can change how people interact in the environment. Evidence shows such interventions reduce gun violence. They also have the potential to improve residents' mental and social well-being.

Invest in Underserved Communities and Populations

Besides changing the physical environment, interventions that invest in whole communities or populations address the underlying causes of gun violence. These interventions can help prevent gun injuries and deaths. Prevention is a strategy that doctors like pediatrician Melissa Dennison understand well. In early 2022 the Kentucky doctor listened as her fourteen-year-old patient described being depressed. The dark-haired girl

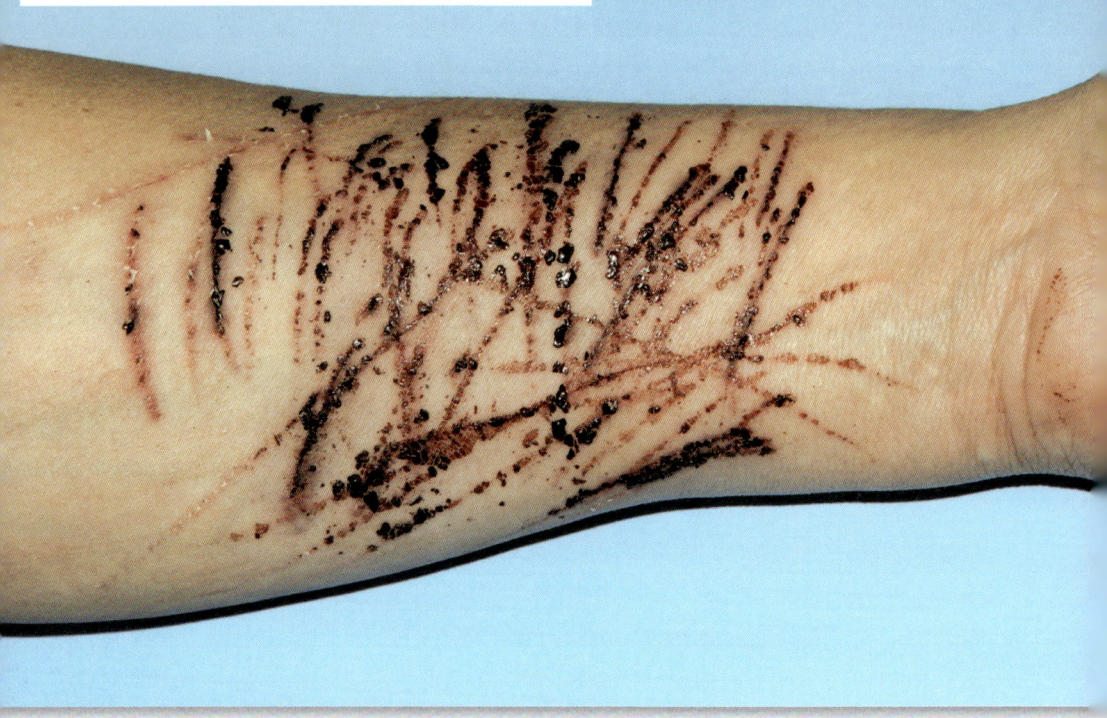

Watching for signs of depression, such as self-harm, is important for preventing suicide. Medical professionals can recognize certain behaviors and intervene using such methods as prescribing antidepressants.

with the Purple Rain T-shirt had been cutting her arm, reporter Matt Richtel writes, in an ineffective and harmful attempt to cope with her depression. Dennison wanted to refer the teen to a psychiatrist, but the waiting list for mental health professionals in the area was a month long. She knows the risks of delay. Kentucky's gun suicide rate is almost 60 percent higher than the national rate. She prescribed the teen an antidepressant.

Substance abuse, depression, and other severe mental health disorders raise the risk for violence, especially suicide. Therapy and medications can improve poor mental health, but many areas lack facilities and providers. Rural areas face particularly high shortages. Fewer than 40 percent of the most rural counties have a mental health care facility, according to research led by nursing professor Janessa Graves. Difficulties affording care and the fear of stigmatization also prevent people from seeking help. Some research finds that increasing access to mental health care—for example, by opening additional facilities or covering treatment costs—corresponds with reductions in violence.

Other interventions focus on populations rather than places. Youth are one population often targeted. Young people perpetrate and fall victim to interpersonal gun violence at the highest rates. Interventions that keep youth busy and help them develop skills and healthy relationships can curb violence. The One Summer Chicago program, for example, provides summer jobs and mentors to teens from high-violence public high schools in Chicago. One study found that the program reduced violent arrests by 42 percent in a year. Summer job programs for teens have also reduced violent crime arrests in Boston and New York. Other place- or population-based interventions associated with reduced violence include those that increase the duration or quality of schools, the availability of high-quality after-school programming, and the affordability of housing. Place- and population-based programs can take years to impact the rates of violence, but just like changes to cars and roads, these interventions can ultimately save lives.

Pros and Cons of Changing Environments to Reduce Gun Violence

Rather than focusing on specific high-risk individuals, some gun violence interventions target places or populations. Changing individuals' behaviors directly can be hard, maybe more difficult than changing the structures and resources that shape behavior. Unlike gun laws, many of these interventions are uncontroversial. Creating pocket parks, providing mental health resources, and keeping kids in school receive support from people with different political views. In communities where trust in police is low, combining nonpolice alternatives with improved policing may address gun crime most effectively. In addition, interventions like expanded access to mental health care, jobs

Reducing Violence Through High-Quality Preschool Education

Young children who attend a high-quality preschool program grow up to commit violence at lower rates than other children. This is another example of how environment shapes individuals' behavior. In a famous study of early education, the High/Scope Perry Preschool project, young children from low-income families were randomly assigned to receive two years of a high-quality preschool education or not. The intervention did not just boost educational achievement, it also reduced violence. By age nineteen, students who attended the program had significantly lower incidents of violent behavior. By age forty, the former preschoolers had many fewer arrests for violent crime. Two percent had been arrested for a violent felony, compared to 12 percent of people who had not attended the program. How does early childhood education reduce violent crime in adulthood? There is no single or certain explanation, but high-quality preschool programs teach self-control and social skills, support the development of healthy relationships with adults and peers, promote later academic achievement, and help reduce aggression. These are factors that help prevent involvement in gun violence.

for youth, high-quality schools, and affordable housing deliver benefits beyond reductions in violence. These interventions can improve mental, social, and economic well-being. They also begin to redress policies that have chronically drained resources from communities of color.

Programs that target places and populations can work, but they do not always do so. Success depends on multiple factors, including the quality of the implementation, consistent funding, and what alternatives exist. Many also take time. Crime researcher Thomas Abt compares the urban community gun violence problem to a gunshot victim in the emergency room: "First you stop the bleeding, because unless you stop the bleeding, nothing else matters."[36] Residents of communities where gunshots erupt regularly cannot wait years for a solution. Neither can victims of ongoing domestic violence, people wrestling with suicidal thoughts, or students planning escape routes from their classrooms just in case a shooter appears.

Gun violence has multiple forms, causes, and consequences. Baltimore mayor Brandon Scott says solutions must be equally complex. Gun violence has "had a hold on my city for longer than I've been breathing oxygen," Scott says. "What folks want to rush to is there's one cause or one thing—one action and one solution. And what we know from living here is that there is no quick fix."[37] Solving gun violence requires multiple, layered solutions. Passing new gun safety laws and enforcing current laws can directly reduce the shooting, but both approaches are politically difficult. Law enforcement must be part of the solution, but law enforcement comes with a high financial cost and can strain community-police relationships when it is not fairly implemented. Interventions and investments that target high-risk individuals, places, or populations address underlying causes and in some cases help address long-standing social injustices. But these solutions often take time and depend on funding, commitment, and other resources that too often come in spurts. While none of these solutions is enough, layering them could make a powerful difference.

Gun ownership is a right that most Americans support. Most Americans also support doing something more about gun violence. The day after nineteen children and two adults were shot and killed at Robb Elementary School in Uvalde, Texas, journalist Nicholas Kristof wrote, "We're tired of commemorating gun violence in America *only* with thoughts and prayers. We didn't respond to Russia's invasion of Ukraine *simply* with thoughts and prayers, or to the 9/11 attacks *only* with moments of silence."[38] Both gun owners and nonowners agree that more must be done. Reducing gun violence is about saving lives, stemming trauma, and supporting social justice.

> "We're tired of commemorating gun violence in America *only* with thoughts and prayers. We didn't respond to Russia's invasion of Ukraine *simply* with thoughts and prayers, or to the 9/11 attacks *only* with moments of silence."[38]
>
> —Nicholas Kristof, journalist

SOURCE NOTES

Introduction: Moving Beyond Gun Politics

1. Quoted in Charlotte Alter, "The Education of David Hogg," *Time*, July 4/July 11, 2022, p. 14.
2. Quoted in Alter, "The Education of David Hogg," p. 15.
3. David Hogg, "Mass Shootings Can Be Stopped Only If We Work Together," Fox News, June 10, 2022. www.foxnews.com.
4. Quoted in Jennifer Mascia and Olga Pierce, "Youth Gun Suicide Is Rising, Particularly Among Children of Color," The Trace, February 24, 2022. www.thetrace.org.

Chapter One: The Gun Violence Problem

5. Quoted in Tiana Woodard, "Annual Mother's Day Walk for Peace Hits the Streets Again After Two Years of Virtual Events," *Boston Globe*, May 8, 2022. www.bostonglobe.com.
6. Quoted in Thomas Abt, *Bleeding Out: The Devastating Consequences of Urban Violence—and a Bold New Plan for Peace in the Streets*. New York: Basic Books, 2019, p. 17.
7. Quoted in Deidre McPhillips, "US Suicide Rates Rose in 2021, Reversing Two Years of Decline," CNN, September 30, 2022. www.cnn.com.
8. Quoted in Keith Coffman, "Colorado Police Say Suspect Who Killed Six at Party Had 'Control Issues,'" Reuters, May 11, 2021. www.reuters.com.
9. Quoted in Jonah Meadows, "Highland Park Shooting Survivor Cooper Roberts Returns Home from Rehab," Patch, September 22, 2022. https://patch.com.
10. Quoted in Peter Hermann and Perry Stein, "'When It's a Shooting on a City Street, Nothing Happens,'" *Washington Post*, June 6, 2022. www.washingtonpost.com.
11. Abt, *Bleeding Out*, p. 18.

Chapter Two: Limit Access to Guns Through Additional Legislation

12. Quoted in NBC News, *Texas Gov. Abbott Holds Press Conference on Uvalde Elementary School Shooting*, YouTube, May 25, 2022. www.youtube.com/watch?v=2TGoreFWJH8.

13. J.B. Pritzker (@GovPritzker), "You are lying about Chicago and what actually perpetuates gun violence. The majority of guns used in Chicago shootings come from states with lax gun laws," Twitter, May 25, 2022, 2:04 pm. https://twitter.com/GovPritzker/status/1529538989140623361.

14. Quoted in *Time*, *Senator Chris Murphy Asks Colleagues "Why Are We Here" in a Speech After Texas School Shooting*, YouTube, May 24, 2022. www.youtube.com/watch?v=30cZDNKJdyU.

15. Quoted in CBS Los Angeles, *Raw Video: Golden State Warriors Coach Steve Kerr Reacts to the Shooting in Uvalde, Texas*, YouTube, May 25, 2022. www.youtube.com/watch?v=gPB8JDbRw-E.

16. Quoted in Gene Johnson and Associated Press, "When It Comes to Gun Purchases, Just 9 States and D.C. Have Waiting Periods. Among Those Who Don't: the Federal Government," *Fortune*, June 5, 2022. https://fortune.com.

17. John Woodrow Cox et al., "In America, a Child Is Shot Every Hour, and Hundreds Die. Here Are 13 Young Lives Lost in 2021," *Washington Post*, January 12, 2022. www.washingtonpost.com.

18. Caroline Light, "A 'Stand Your Ground' Expansion That Expands Inequality," *New York Times*, March 23, 2017. www.nytimes.com.

Chapter Three: Improve the Enforcement of Gun Laws

19. Quoted in Jennifer Gollan, "How the US Fails to Take Away Guns from Domestic Abusers: 'These Deaths Are Preventable.'" *The Guardian* (Manchester, UK), October 26, 2021. www.theguardian.com.

20. Quoted in *Seattle Times* Editorial Board, "New Seattle–King County Task Force Makes Gun Laws Work," *Seattle Times*, March 3, 2018. www.seattletimes.com.

21. Quoted in Nicole Narea, "New York's Restrictive Gun Laws Didn't Stop the Buffalo Shooter," Vox, May 18, 2022. www.vox.com.

22. Quoted in Bernard Condon, "Red Flag Laws Get Little Use as Shootings, Gun Deaths Soar," Associated Press, September 2, 2022. https://apnews.com.

23. Quoted in CNN, "Guns in America Town Hall with Obama Transcript (Full Text)," CNN, January 7, 2016. www.cnn.com.

24. Abt, *Bleeding Out*, p. 74.

Chapter Four: Implement Intervention Programs Targeting High-Risk Individuals

25. Gary Slutkin, *Let's Treat Violence like a Contagious Disease*, TED, 2013. www.ted.com/talks/gary_slutkin_let_s_treat_violence_like_a_contagious_disease.
26. Quoted in Chicago CRED, "Coaching & Counseling." www.chicagocred.org.
27. Quoted in Samantha Michaels, "Whose Streets?," *Mother Jones*, September/October 2020. www.motherjones.com.
28. Stephen R. Band and Joseph A. Harpold, "School Violence: Lessons Learned," *FBI Law Enforcement Bulletin*, September 1999. https://leb.fbi.gov.
29. Mark Follman. *Trigger Points: Inside the Mission to Stop Mass Shootings in America*. New York: Dey Street, 2022, p. 16.
30. Quoted in John Woodrow Cox, *Children Under Fire: An American Crisis*. New York: Ecco, 2022, p. 44.

Chapter Five: Change the Environment to Change Behavior

31. Jason E. Goldstick et al., "Current Causes of Death in Children and Adolescents in the United States," *New England Journal of Medicine* 386, no. 20 (May 2022), p. 1956.
32. David Hemenway and Matthew Miller, "Counterpoint: Reducing Firearm Violence—Why a Public Health Approach Is Helpful," *Journal of Policy Analysis and Management* 38, no. 3 (2019), p. 796.
33. Quoted in Chicago CRED, "Coaching & Counseling."
34. Quoted in Sonali Rajan, "Cleaning and Greening: Episode Transcription," *Research for Solutions*, December 9, 2019. https://researchforsolutions.com.
35. Quoted in *JAMA Internal Medicine Author Interviews*, "Abandoned Housing Interventions and Gun Violence, Perceptions of Safety, and Substance Use," December 5, 2022. https://jamanetwork.com.
36. Abt, *Bleeding Out*, p. 1.
37. Quoted in Juana Summers, "In Baltimore's Streets, Interrupters Face Danger to Stop a Cycle of Violence," NPR, February 13, 2022. www.npr.org.
38. Nicholas Kristof, "These Gun Reforms Could Save 15,000 Lives. We Can Achieve Them," *New York Times*, May 25, 2022. www.nytimes.com.

FOR FURTHER RESEARCH

Books

Thomas Abt, *Bleeding Out: The Devastating Consequences of Urban Violence—and a Bold New Plan for Peace in the Streets*. New York: Basic Books, 2019.

John Woodrow Cox, *Children Under Fire: An American Crisis*. New York: Ecco, 2022.

Dave Cullen, *Parkland: Birth of a Movement*. New York: Harper-Collins, 2019.

Mark Follman, *Trigger Points: Inside the Mission to Stop Mass Shootings in America*. New York: Dey Street, 2022.

Michelle Roehm McCann and Shannon Watts, *Enough Is Enough: How Students Can Join the Fight for Gun Safety*. New York: Simon Pulse, 2019.

Internet Resources

American Psychological Association, "Gun Violence: Prediction, Prevention, and Policy," 2013. www.apa.org.

John Jay College Research Advisory Group on Preventing and Reducing Community Violence, *Reducing Violence Without Police: A Review of Research Evidence*. New York: John Jay College of Criminal Justice Research and Evaluation Center, 2021. https://johnjayrec.nyc.

Johns Hopkins Center for Gun Violence Solutions, *A Year in Review: 2020 Gun Deaths in the U.S.* Baltimore: Johns Hopkins Bloomberg School of Public Health, 2022. https://publichealth .jhu.edu.

Rosanna Smart et al., *The Science of Gun Policy: A Critical Synthesis of Research Evidence on the Effects of Gun Policies in the United States*. Santa Monica, CA: RAND Corporation, 2020. www.rand.org.

Websites

Giffords Law Center to Prevent Gun Violence

https://giffords.org/lawcenter

The Giffords Law Center to Prevent Gun Violence is a gun safety advocacy organization started by former congresswoman Gabrielle Giffords after she was injured in a mass shooting. The center's website provides detailed information about gun laws by state and type of policy. It also tracks gun-related legislation.

Gun Violence Archive

www.gunviolencearchive.org

The Gun Violence Archive collects data from over seventy-five hundred sources, including local law enforcement agencies and media, about shooting incidents. The website, updated daily, includes tables, maps, and a spreadsheet that lists shootings by date, location, and number of casualties.

Pew Research Center, Gun Policy

www.pewresearch.org/topic/politics-policy/political-issues/gun-policy

The Pew Research Center is a nonpartisan, not-for-profit research organization known best for its opinion surveys. It covers a wide range of political topics, including frequent surveys and reports that show what Americans think about gun violence and gun policy.

The Trace

www.thetrace.org

The Trace is a nonprofit news site focused exclusively on gun violence. Its articles cover all forms of gun violence; they range from basic information to in-depth analyses of the causes of gun violence.

INDEX

Note: Boldface page numbers indicate illustrations.

Abbott, Greg, 17
Abt, Thomas, 7, 16, 33, 37, 54
Alter, Charlotte, 4
American Academy of Pediatrics, 49
American Federation of Teachers, 25
assault-weapons bans, 22–23

background checks, 20–21
Barnhorst, Amy, 6
behavioral threat assessment, 40–44
    anonymous tip lines and, 43
Bipartisan Safer Communities Act (2022), 6, 18, 40
Black American(s)
    communities, building trust between police and, 32–33
    males, as percentage of all gun homicides, 9
    police killings of, 11
    racial bias in application of law and, 24
Brady: United Against Gun Violence, 31
Branas, Charles, 49–50
Buffalo grocery store shooting (2022), 11, 29, **30**
Bureau of Alcohol, Tobacco, Firearms and Explosives (ATF), 26, 31–32

car crash fatalities, decline in, 46–47
Carter, Patrick, 47
Caught in the Crossfire program, 37–38

Centers for Disease Control and Prevention (CDC), 5, 8, 46
Chicago Police Department, 9
child-access-prevention laws, 23–24
Clayton, Shanae, 26
community violence interruption programs, 37–39
Cooper, Anderson, **34**
Cruz, Nikolas, 15
Cunningham, Rebecca, 47
Cure Violence program, 37, 39, 41, **41**

deaths
    from car crashes, 46
    firearm, 8, 9, 11
Dennison, Melissa, 51–52
Desmond, Matthew, 32
Dickey Amendment (1996), 22
disarming, of prohibited possessors, 27–28
domestic violence, 10
    children exposed to, as risk factor for gun violence, 16
    conviction for, as cause for gun restrictions, 19–20, 25, 27–28

Federal Bureau of Alcohol, Tobacco, Firearms and Explosives (ATF), 31–32
firearms
    gun violence and access to, 15
    people prohibited from owning, 27
Follman, Mark, 41, 42
Freilich, Ari, 8
Fryer, Kadeem, 31

Gendron, Payton, 29
Giffords Law Center to Prevent Gun Violence, 19, 25, 60

61

Goldstick, Jason E., 47
Graves, Janessa, 52
Green, Keith, 47–49
gun industry, use of civil law against, 33
gun laws
    categories of, 18
    controlling carrying, storage, or use, 23–24
    difficulty in enacting, 25
    jurisdictions refusing to enforce, 29
    limiting ownership, 18–20
    regulating sales/transfers, 20–23
    support for strengthening, 17–18
Gun Policy in America initiative (RAND), 18
gun storage
    changing norms for, 46
    safe, laws requiring, 23–24
gun violence
    economic consequences of, 14–15
    forms of, 5, 12
    as leading cause of death among American youth, 46
    research on, limits on federal spending for, 22
    risk factors for, 15–16
Gun Violence Archive, 10, 60

Harris poll, 13
Harvard Medical School, 13
Harvard University, 23
Hemenway, David, 46
Heyne, Christian, 30
Higbee, Joshua, 33
Hogg, David, 4–5, **5**
homicides, gun-related
    in 2021, **11**
    high-risk groups for, 12
    red flag laws and, 20
    stand-your-ground laws linked to, 24
    waiting periods and, 22
Hudnall, DaMya, 23

Ibarra-Perez, Sandra, 10
injuries/trauma, 12–13
    economic cost of, 14
intervention/intervention programs
    behavioral threat assessment, 42–44

community-based, 37–40
pros and cons of, 45
targeting high-risk individuals, 36–37
targeting physical environment, 47–51

Jackson, Alvoncia, 13
John Jay College of Criminal Justice, 39
Johns Hopkins University, 9
Jude, Frank, Jr., 32

Kerr, Steve, 20, **21**
Kristof, Nicholas, 55
Kunard, Laura, 33–34

Langman, Peter, 41–42
Lasley, James, 51
Light, Caroline, 24

Marjory Stoneman Douglas High School shooting (FL, 2021), 15
mass shooting(s), 4, 10–11, 12
    behavioral threat assessment and, 37, 41–42, 44
    definition of, 10
    hearing about, as source of stress, 13
Medley, Miayon, 36
Miller, Matthew, 46
Milwaukee Journal Sentinel (newspaper), 32
Moe, Charlene, 33–34
Murphy, Chris, 18, 20

Nanasi, Natalie, 26, 27
National Center for Education Statistics, 43
National Center for Injury Prevention and Control, 13
National Highway Traffic Safety Administration, 46
National Threat Assessment Center, 43
New York Times (newspaper), 11
Northeastern University, 23
Novick, Dorothy R., 49

Obama, Barack, 32, **34**
Odom, Kim, 7–8

62

Omdia, 12
One Summer Chicago program, 53
Operation Ceasefire program, 39
Operation Cul-de-Sac (Los Angeles
    Police Department), 51
opinion polls. *See* surveys

Page, Johnny, 47
Papachristos, Andrew, 37, 40
Paredes, Sam, 22
permit-to-purchase laws, 22
Pew Research Center, 60
police
    building trust between underserved
        communities and, 32–35
    deaths from shootings by, 11
polls. *See* surveys
poverty, as risk factor for gun violence,
    16
Pritzker, J.B., 17
procedural justice, 33–34
protective factors, 16

RAND, 18, 20, 21, 22, 23–24, 30
Reams, Steve, 29
red flag laws, 19, 26, 29
    are rarely used, 30–31
    uncertain impact of, 20
Richtel, Matt, 52
Roberts, Cooper, 12–13
Roberts, Jason, 13
Roberts, Keely, 13
Roca (outreach program), 36

Safer Families, Safer Communities,
    28
Safe2Tell program (CO), 43
Sandy Hook Elementary School
    shooting (CT, 2012), 18
Satterberg, Dan, 28
school security, cost of, 12
Second Amendment Preservation Act
    (MO), 29
Second Amendment sanctuaries, 29
Slutkin, Gary, 37

South, Eugenia, 50–51
stand-your-ground laws, 23, 24
    effectiveness of repealing, 25
straw purchases, 31
suicide, 8
    gun-related, in 2021, **11**
    high-risk groups for, 12
    mental health disorders and, 15–16
    waiting periods and, 22
surveys
    on importance of reducing gun
        violence, 5
    on protection of gun rights, 5
    on stress from news about gun
        violence, 13
    on support for stricter gun laws,
        17–18
    of teachers on being armed, 25
Swanson, Jeffrey, 30

teachers, arming of, 25
The Trace (website), 29, 32, 60
trauma, 12–13
    as risk factor for gun violence, 16

underserved communities
    building trust between police and,
        32–35
    importance of investing in, 51–53
    intervention programs targeting,
        37–40
Urban Institute, 14
USA Today (newspaper), 32
Uvalde elementary school shooting
    (TX, 2022), 17, **19**

violence interrupters, 38, **38**, 40, 45

waiting periods, 21–22
Washington Post (newspaper), 11, 23
Washington State Coalition Against
    Domestic Violence, 27
Webster, Daniel, 22
West, Jamal, 36
Whatley, Demeatreas, **41**

PICTURE CREDITS

Cover: MyImages-Micha/Shutterstock.com

5: Phillip Yabut/Shutterstock.com

11: Maury Aaseng

14: Peter Titmuss/Alamy Stock Photo

19: Bob Daemmrich/Alamy Stock Photo

21: Sipa USA/Alamy Stock Photo

28: Jim West/Alamy Stock Photo

30: Reuters/Alamy Stock Photo

34: Aude Guerrucci/dpa/picture-alliance/Newscom

38: Associated Press

41: Associated Press

44: Lopolo/Shutterstock.com

48: Branislav Nenin/Shutterstock.com

50: Jim West/Alamy Stock Photo

52: Dr P. Marazzi/Science Photo Library